BUILDING BLOCKS OF GEOGRAPHY

EARTH'S PROCESSES AND CHANGES

Written by Izzi Howell

Illustrated by Steve Evans

WORLD BOOK

a Scott Fetzer company
Chicago

World Book, Inc.
180 North LaSalle Street
Suite 900
Chicago, Illinois 60601
USA

For information about other World Book publications,
visit our website at **www.worldbook.com**
or call **1-800-WORLDBK (967-5325).**
For information about sales to schools and libraries,
call 1-800-975-3250 (United States),
or 1-800-837-5365 (Canada).

Library of Congress Cataloging-in-Publication Data
for this volume has been applied for.

Building Blocks of Geography
ISBN: 978-0-7166-4275-6 (set, hc.)

Earth's Processes and Changes
ISBN: 978-0-7166-4279-4 (hc.)

Also available as:
ISBN: 978-0-7166-4289-3 (e-book)

1st printing June 2022

WORLD BOOK STAFF
Executive Committee
President: Geoff Broderick
Vice President, Editorial: Tom Evans
Vice President, Finance: Donald D. Keller
Vice President, Marketing: Jean Lin
Vice President, International: Eddy Kisman
Vice President, Technology: Jason Dole
Director, Human Resources: Bev Ecker

Editorial
Manager, New Content: Jeff De La Rosa
Associate Manager, New Product:
    Nicholas Kilzer
Sr. Editor: Shawn Brennan
Proofreader: Nathalie Strassheim

Graphics and Design
Sr. Visual Communications Designer:
    Melanie Bender
Sr. Web Designer/Digital Media Developer:
    Matt Carrington
Coordinator, Design Development:
    Brenda Tropinski

Acknowledgments:
Writer: Izzi Howell
Illustrator: Steve Evans
Series advisor: Marjorie Frank

Developed with World Book by
White-Thomson Publishing LTD

www.wtpub.co.uk

TABLE OF CONTENTS

There is a glossary on page 40. Terms defined in the glossary are in type **that looks like this** on their first appearance.

CHANGING EARTH

After about 200 million years, I formed a crust and oceans. The gigantic plates that form my crust are constantly moving.
As a result, over millions of years, entire continents move apart or crash into each other. Mountains form and seas and oceans appear.
This is how I looked 200 million years ago. Quite different, huh? I can barely recognize myself.
In 200 million years' time, I'm sure I'll have changed just as much again!

It's hard to believe but rain and wind can change the shape of rock.
The weather can change my surface. This is called physical weathering.
Physical weathering is the wearing down or breaking up of rocks through contact with water, wind, and temperature changes.

Hello there, Water and Rock! Let's see which of you is stronger.

Water can collect in a crack in Rock.

If I freeze and turn into ice, my volume increases by around 9 percent. As ice, I expand and push the crack apart.
If the ice thaws, more water can get in and the process repeats, making the crack bigger. This is freeze-thaw weathering.

It may seem surprising, but in this way, Water is stronger than Rock.

Temperature changes can also cause physical weathering. I expand in the heat...
...and get smaller in the cold.

This causes cracks to form in me. Freeze-thaw weathering can make these cracks bigger.

Wind can cause physical weathering by blowing sand grains or small bits of dirt or rock against me, gradually wearing me away and changing my shape.

Waves constantly pound the coasts. The beaches and cliffs you see today are partly a result of millions of years of physical weathering.

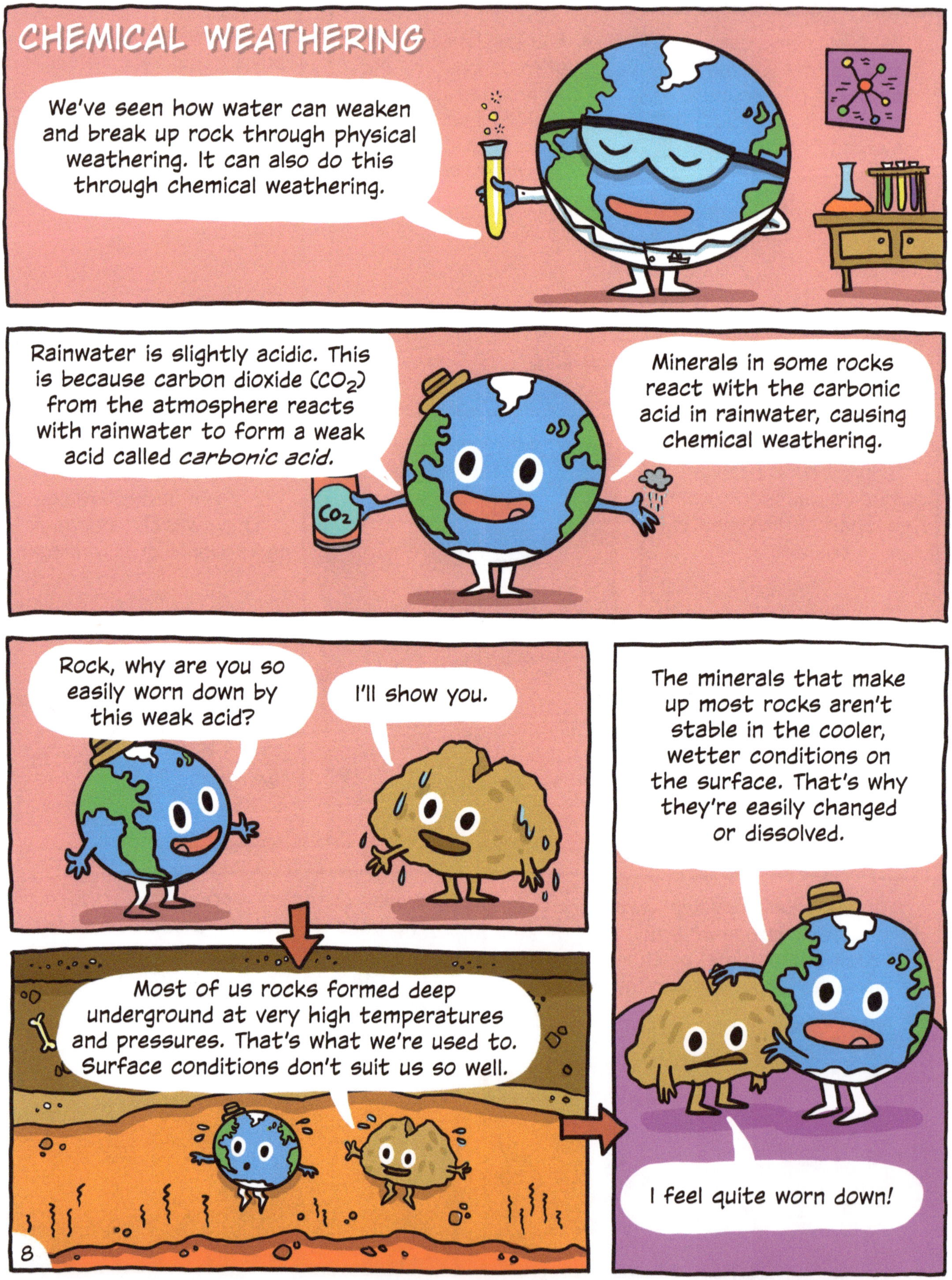

CHEMICAL WEATHERING

Caves form when carbonic acid in rainwater eats into limestone, forming large fissures underground, usually around the level of the water table.

STALACTITE
STALAGMITE
When the carbonic acid reacts with limestone, minerals from the stone dissolve in the water. This mineral-laden water drips into a cave, gradually forming stalactites and stalagmites.

Oxygen in water also reacts with iron in some rocks to form iron oxide (rust). Iron oxide is weaker than iron so this helps wear away the rock. You're looking a bit red, Rock!

Sometimes water itself, not the chemicals within it, can dissolve minerals in rock. For example, water reacts with crystals inside granite to form clay. The clay weakens the rock, making it more likely to break.
I feel quite de-feet-ed!

BIOLOGICAL WEATHERING
Cute, isn't he? You wouldn't think he'd harm a fly, let alone a rock. Yet he and other burrowing animals can do a great deal to weaken and break up rocks.

It's just a little plant, right? What damage could it possibly do to a rock? A surprising amount!
Biological weathering is the wearing down and breaking up of rocks by plants and animals.

A burrowing animal can burrow into a crack in me, making it bigger.

Badgers break up rock underground and bring it to the surface where it is exposed to physical and chemical weathering.

If a tree or plant sends its roots into a crack, it can put great pressure on a rock and even cause it to split.

Some living things can cause chemical weathering. Lichen is a living thing made up of fungi and another organism—usually algae.
The fungi release chemicals that break down minerals in the rock. The algae use these minerals for nutrition. Removing the minerals weakens the rock and exposes it to other types of weathering.

Physical, chemical, and biological weathering all work together to weaken and break up rocks.

Weathering breaks rock down into tiny particles called sediment. Common examples of sediment include gravel, silt, clay, and sand.

Without the sediments produced by weathering, there would be no soil and therefore no plants. Without plants there would be no animals or humans.

Weathering is therefore one reason why there's life on Earth. So, thank you, Rock!
You're welcome!

EROSION AND DEPOSITION

Rain can wash me into rivers and streams. Glug!

Eventually, my journey has to end when I'm deposited, or built up, on a landmass. This is called deposition.

I might become a desert sand dune...

Or a river bed...

After millions of years, pressure and time might turn me into sedimentary rock.

Hi!
It's hard to imagine rain as something that can change the landscape.
But rain can cause serious erosion—especially when it's heavy. Here's my friend Fresh Water to explain how.
Each raindrop hits the soil, making its mark. This is called splash erosion.
If it's raining hard, the raindrop creates a small hollow in the soil, ejecting soil particles. This is fun!

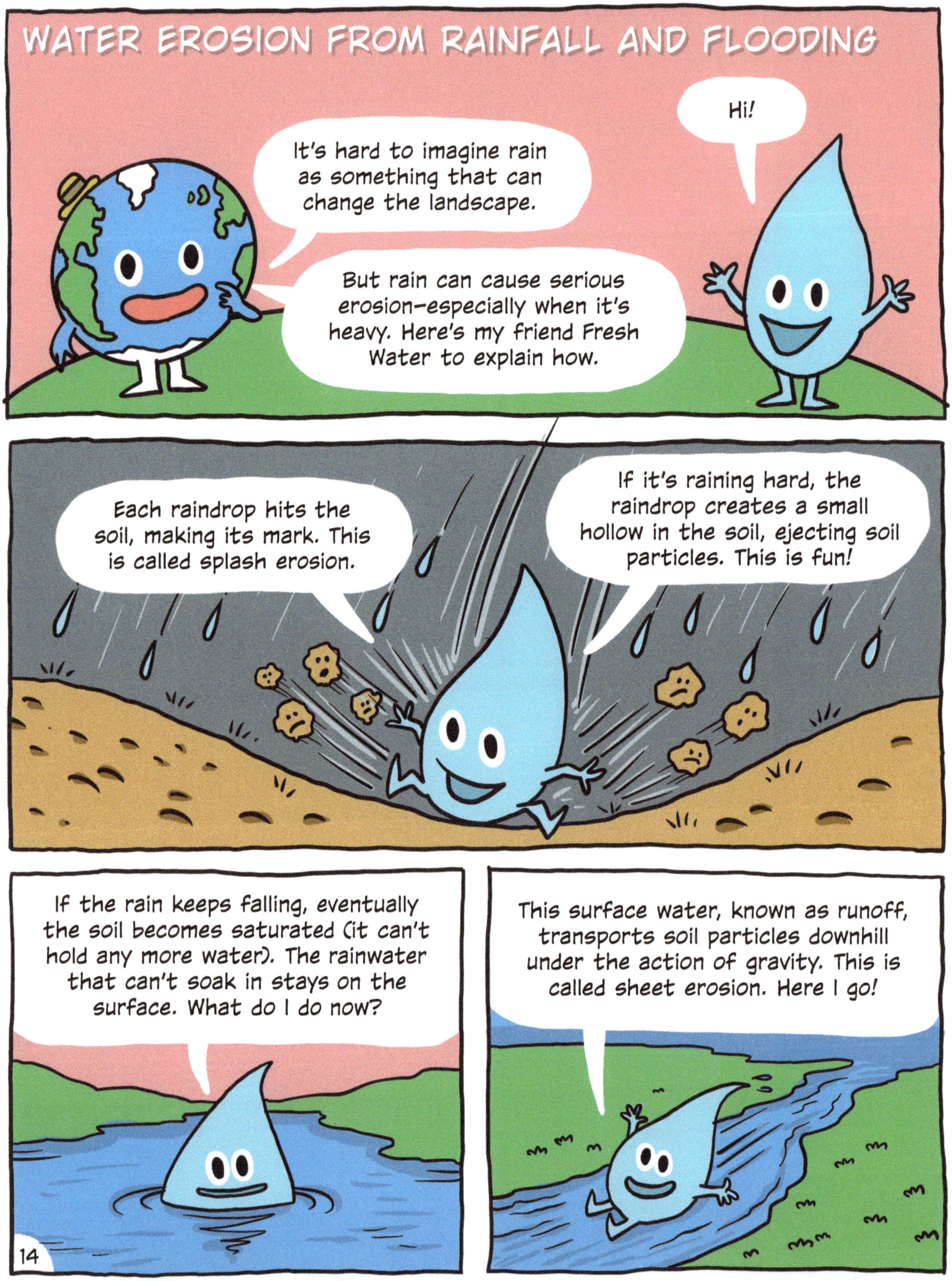

If the rain keeps falling, eventually the soil becomes saturated (it can't hold any more water). The rainwater that can't soak in stays on the surface. What do I do now?

This surface water, known as runoff, transports soil particles downhill under the action of gravity. This is called sheet erosion. Here I go!

As it flows downhill, the water starts to form small channels in the soil called rills. Water flows faster along rills and can detach and transport more soil.

When there's a lot of runoff due to heavy rains or melting snow, rills may develop into gullies. These are bigger, deeper channels that cause even more soil erosion.
Now I'm really changing the landscape!

This rain is seriously heavy now!

Sometimes heavy rains and storms can lead to flash floods. These can cause rapid soil erosion.

Erosion from rainfall and flash floods can be damaging to farmland if it removes topsoil—the fertile upper layer of soil.

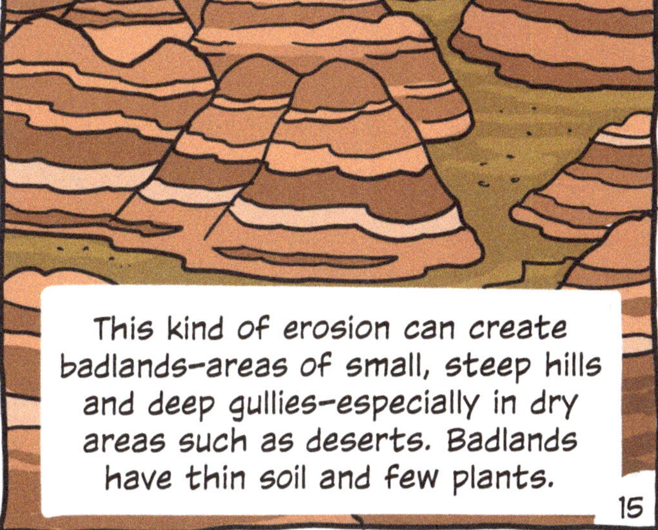
This kind of erosion can create badlands—areas of small, steep hills and deep gullies—especially in dry areas such as deserts. Badlands have thin soil and few plants.

WATER EROSION FROM RIVERS

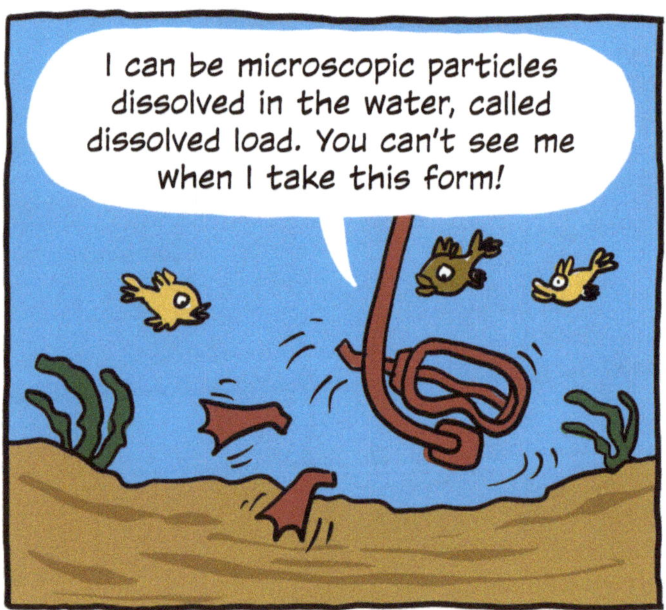

Hey, this is fast! The river starts high in the mountains. The **gradient** here is steep and the water flows quickly, eroding the land vertically and cutting a deep, V-shaped channel.

Lots of bends here!

As the river moves lower, the gradient becomes less steep. The river slows and may develop curves called meanders. It now erodes more material from its **banks** and less from its bed.

As the river moves onto flatter ground, it slows right down. It erodes the outer banks of its meanders and deposits sediment on the inner banks, creating a snakelike pattern.

When the river floods, it deposits its sediment to create a flat *flood plain*, with fertile soil perfect for farming.

Looks like the end of the journey!

Eventually, the river meets a larger body of water, such as an ocean. Sometimes this causes it to spread out of its channel and expand in width.

At the river's mouth, the river slows, causing it to deposit its sediment. This may build up to form a triangle-shaped plain called a delta. Deltas have fertile soil, ideal for farming.

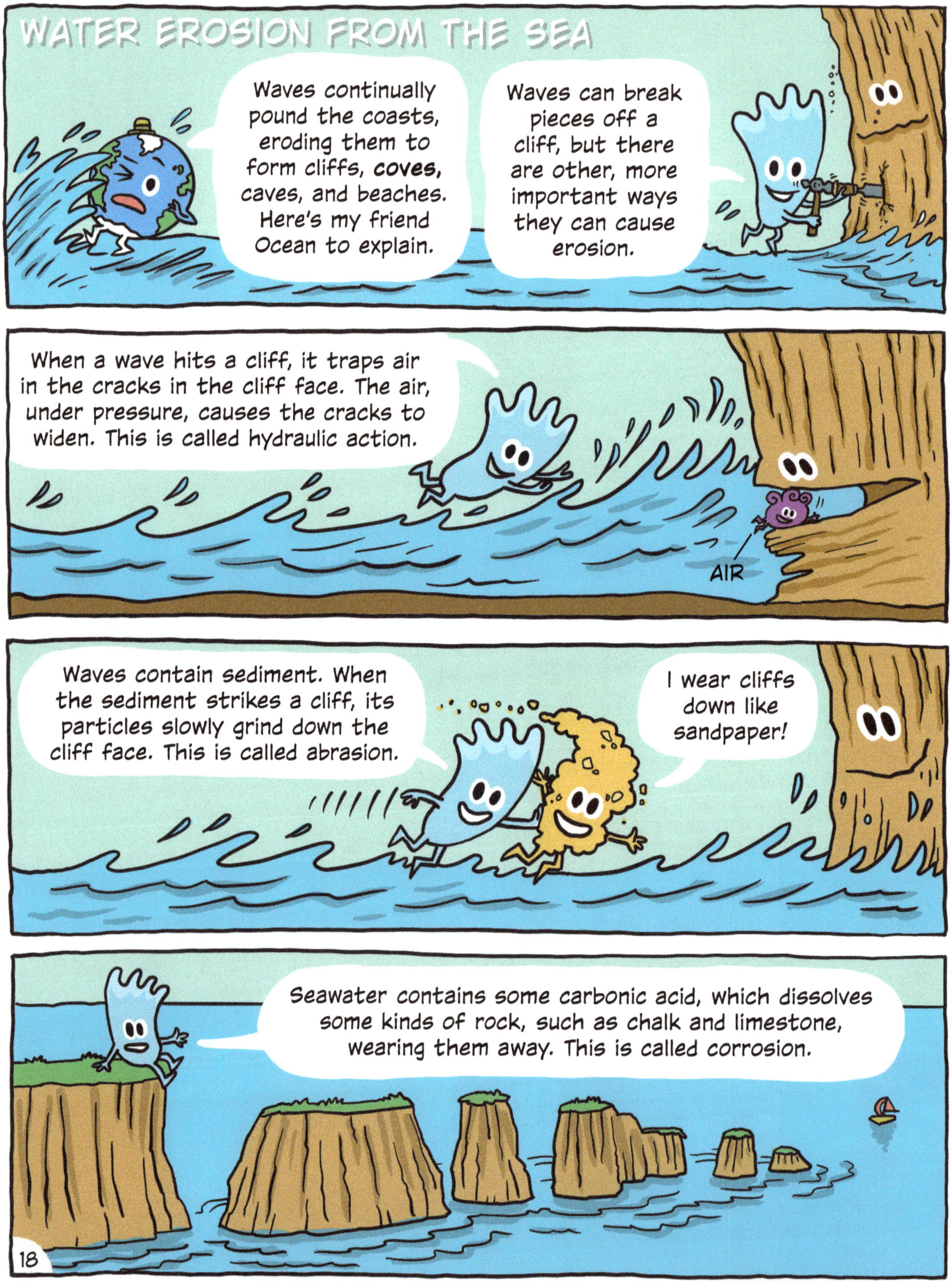

Waves continually pound the coasts, eroding them to form cliffs, **coves**, caves, and beaches. Here's my friend Ocean to explain.
Waves can break pieces off a cliff, but there are other, more important ways they can cause erosion.
When a wave hits a cliff, it traps air in the cracks in the cliff face. The air, under pressure, causes the cracks to widen. This is called hydraulic action.
AIR
Waves contain sediment. When the sediment strikes a cliff, its particles slowly grind down the cliff face. This is called abrasion.
I wear cliffs down like sandpaper!

Seawater contains some carbonic acid, which dissolves some kinds of rock, such as chalk and limestone, wearing them away. This is called corrosion.

The rocky particles carried by the waves smash into each other and the cliffs. This grinds them down, making them smaller and rounder.
They end up as pebble and sand beaches. This is called attrition.
It's like I'm fighting with myself!

When waves lose energy, they drop the sediment they're carrying. This can happen in shallow water, or in a sheltered cove, or where there's little wind.

When waves drop their sediment, it's called coastal deposition, and can lead to the formation of beaches. I'm not complaining!

Coastal deposition can also form a bay bar, when the deposited material blocks off water in a bay. This blocked-off area of water is called a lagoon.
Hey, I'm trapped!

I also transport particles to different places. If I'm not strong enough to lift a particle because it's too big and heavy, I'll slide or roll it along the ground.

I'm taking you guys on a journey!
With very small particles, such as grains of dust or fine sand, I can lift them high into the air and blow them long distances. This is called suspension.

Sometimes, when I blow very hard, I can pull dust from the ground into the air and create a dust storm—a wall of dust and debris that can be miles or kilometers long.

Eventually, I lose power and the particles I'm transporting fall back to the surface. They may end up as sand sheets—flat, gently undulating areas of sand...

Or they form in ripples like this, due to saltation. With ripples, the largest grains end up at the crests. This desert could do with an iron!

Or I might blow them into a mound called a dune. Dunes have gentle slopes on the side facing the wind, and steep slopes on the other side.
With dunes, the largest grains end up in the troughs.

ICE EROSION
Brrrr! I've taken you to a very cold place to learn about erosion by ice.
A glacier is a huge mass of ice that moves slowly over land pulled by gravity. Glaciers form in the polar regions and in mountain ranges.

As a glacier moves, it erodes the land beneath using three different processes: abrasion, plucking, and ice thrusting.

I'm getting quite a scraping here! Bits of rock get caught in the base of a glacier. These work like sandpaper, wearing away the land underneath. This is called abrasion.

At the base of the glacier, friction causes its ice to melt and flow into cracks in the bedrock, where it freezes again. This freeze-thaw action cracks the bedrock and causes chunks of rock to break off.

These chunks of rock freeze to the bottom of the glacier and get carried along. This is called plucking. Bon voyage, Rock!
It looks like I'm off on a journey!

Sometimes the glacier freezes to the ground beneath it, then surges forward, dislodging large sheets of sediment frozen to its base. This is called ice thrusting, and it has produced many lake basins.
Hey!

LATERAL MORAINE
MEDIAL MORAINE
A moraine is material left behind by a moving glacier. As a glacier moves down a mountain valley, it deposits bands of debris on either side, called lateral moraines.
If two glaciers join up, the lateral moraines between them form a medial moraine.

When a glacier stops and starts to melt due to increasing temperatures, it deposits a ridge of debris. This is called a terminal moraine.
It looks like my journey's over!

Before the arrival of a glacier, most mountain valleys have a V shape caused by mountain streams.

Glaciers often widen, deepen, and smooth these to form a U-shaped valley. As I said, glaciers certainly change the landscape!

GRAVITY EROSION
Hello!
Hello Gravity! Gravity is constantly changing my surface by pulling rocks and soil from a higher place to a lower place.

We've already seen how rain and ice cause erosion, but it's really me, Gravity, that powers them both by pulling them downhill.

Another way I cause erosion is through a landslide. This can start when a high wind or an earthquake loosens and dislodges rocks and soil.

Thanks to me they go tumbling downhill, getting faster as they fall and dislodging more debris. Suddenly, it turns into a landslide!
Here we go!
24

Landslides can make massive changes to a landscape. Hillsides can collapse, and lakes can form if rocky material dams a river.

On steep hills, I can sometimes cause a slump. This is when a mass of material moves as a block down a slope, leaving a spoon-shaped depression in the hillside.

Not all landslides are fast. Creeps are slow, steady landslides that happen too gradually to see. Signs of a creep are ripples in the ground and trees with curved trunks.

I help cause avalanches, too. These snow slides can be powerful enough to dislodge rocks, boulders, and other debris, depositing them on lower slopes.

Heavy rains can lead to a mudslide. The saturated soil becomes unstable, and I push it downward in a liquid river of water and mud that carries boulders, trees, and other debris with it.

INTERNAL PROCESSES
So far we've talked about how forces on the surface cause changes to my landscapes. But there's also stuff happening underground that can dramatically affect the way I look.

To help explain, let's take a look inside me.
OCEANIC CRUST
CONTINENTAL CRUST
LITHOSPHERE
MANTLE
OUTER CORE
ASTHENOSPHERE
INNER CORE

Remember how I said my crust is made up of separate plates? These "tectonic plates" move around very slowly on a layer of hot, soft rock in the upper mantle.
The plates interact with each other at their boundaries.

At divergent boundaries, where the plates move apart, magma (molten rock) rises to fill the gap. The magma hardens to form new crust. This mostly happens under the ocean.
MAGMA

Whoa, I'm getting pulled apart! On land, this separation of plates, or rifting, can create valleys and also new seas as ocean waters fill the gap.

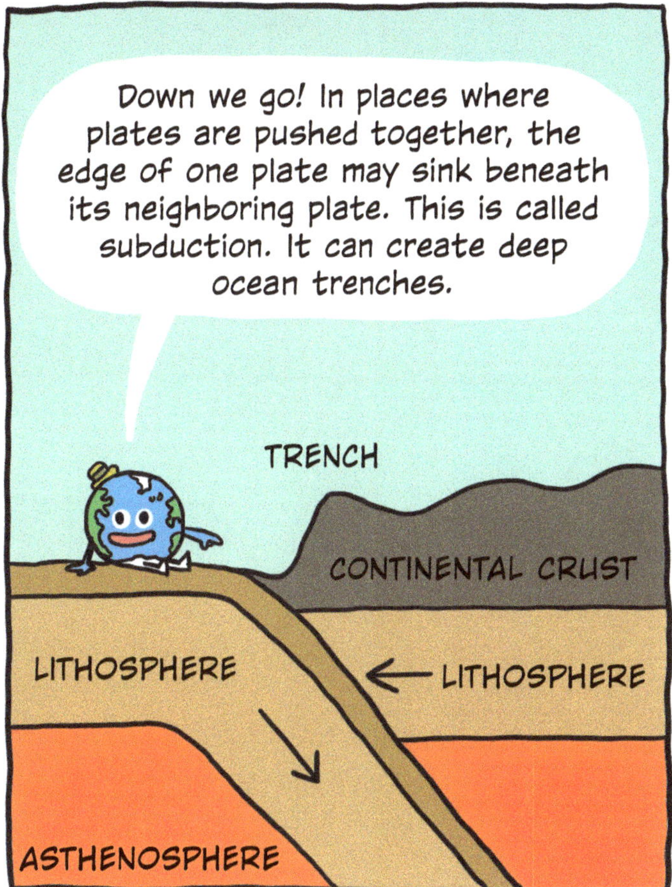

Down we go! In places where plates are pushed together, the edge of one plate may sink beneath its neighboring plate. This is called subduction. It can create deep ocean trenches.
TRENCH
CONTINENTAL CRUST
LITHOSPHERE
LITHOSPHERE
ASTHENOSPHERE

At such convergent boundaries, the overlying plate scrapes sediment off the descending plate. This adds material to the edge of the overlying plate, known as an accretionary wedge.
CONTINENTAL CRUST
ACCRETIONARY WEDGE
LITHOSPHERE
ASTHENOSPHERE

What a collision! When two plates carrying continents collide, layers of rock crumple and fold. This is how the Himalaya mountain range was formed.

VOLCANOES

Excuse me! My internal processes can sometimes produce violent and spectacular results on the surface— such as a volcanic eruption.

Volcanoes are openings in my crust, usually around plate boundaries, through which gases, ash, and molten rock from underground can erupt.

Volcanoes change the look of the landscape in many ways. As they erupt, a hill made of ash, lava, or cinders forms around the vent (opening).

My, you're tall! A stratovolcano is a tall cone made up of layers of lava and ash formed from occasional explosive eruptions over many thousands or millions of years.

A shield volcano is wide and low with gently sloping sides formed from many gentle eruptions of thin, runny lava.

Whoa! That was close! Sometimes blobs of lava hurled into the air by the volcano cool and fall to the ground as pieces of rock called cinders.

The cinders pile up to form a volcano called a cinder cone.

This vent was a lot smaller once! A volcanic vent is surrounded by a bowl-shaped **crater.** After a violent eruption, the top may collapse to form a larger opening called a caldera. Some calderas are huge.

Volcanoes can build spectacular landforms far from the vent through the spread of lava, which turns to rock and can eventually form plateaus covering thousands of square miles or kilometers.
Spectacular, isn't it?

EARTHQUAKES

Uh oh! Earthquakes can have big effects on the landscape. They can trigger landslides, avalanches, mudslides, and slumps.
Undersea earthquakes can create huge, powerful waves called tsunamis.

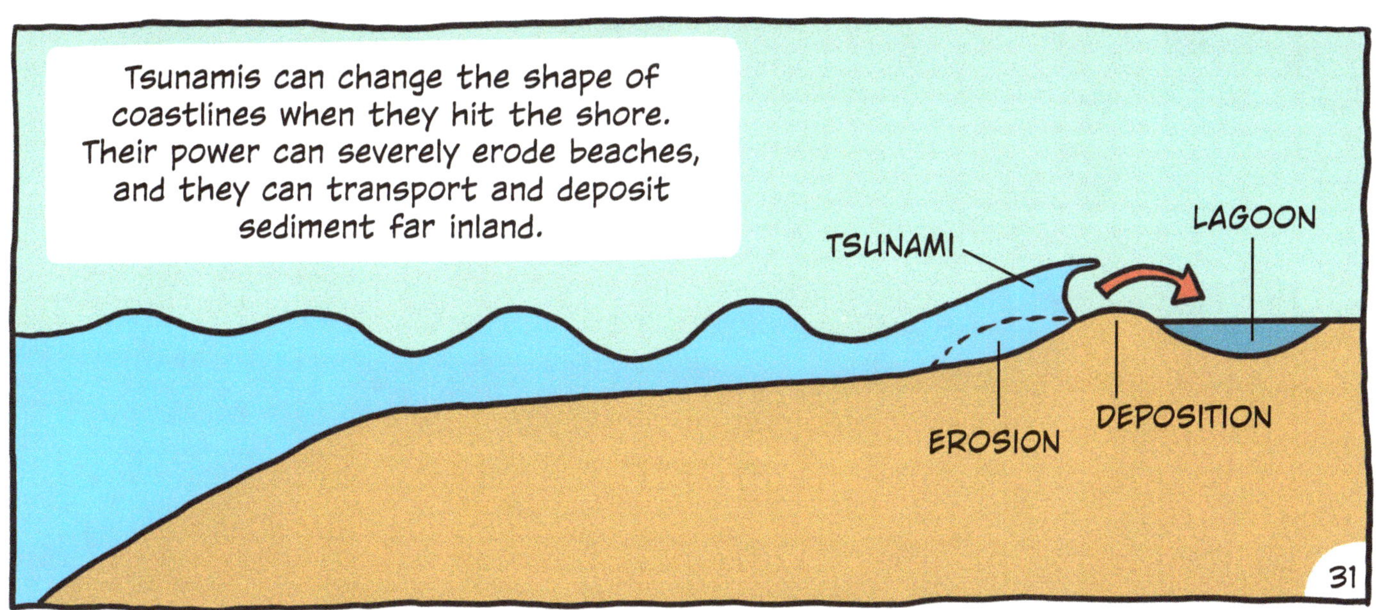
Tsunamis can change the shape of coastlines when they hit the shore. Their power can severely erode beaches, and they can transport and deposit sediment far inland.
TSUNAMI
LAGOON
EROSION
DEPOSITION

HUMAN ACTIVITIES THAT CHANGE EARTH

What a huge hole! Mining companies remove large areas of soil and rock in order to reach an underground mineral deposit.

Sometimes the entire tops of mountains are removed, burying streams and changing the way wind and water erode the remaining landscape.

Sorry Fresh Water! Damming rivers for hydroelectricity greatly affects the local environment. Artificial lakes are formed, while places below the dam can dry up.
I've been blocked off!

Sometimes humans try to stop natural erosion. They protect some coasts by building sea walls and groins, and planting dune grasses around beaches to hold sand in place.
DUNE GRASSES
GROIN
SEA WALL

CLIMATE CHANGE

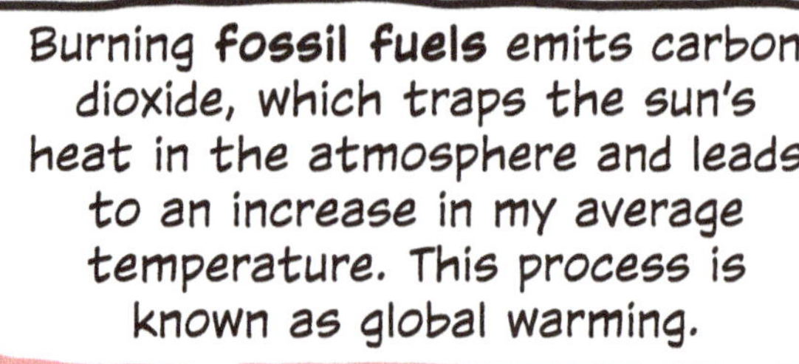

Global warming is affecting the Arctic Ocean. The amount of sea ice that melts there in the summer has increased by around 10 percent each decade since 1978.

Melting ice sheets at the poles and melting mountain glaciers have contributed to a rise in sea levels, endangering low-lying islands and coastlines around the world.

Humans can do something about climate change by changing their behaviors—and reducing their "carbon footprint."

For example, you can switch to renewable forms of energy, such as solar or wind power, instead of using fossil fuels that emit carbon dioxide.

Eating less meat also helps. Cattle produce large amounts of methane, a gas that adds to global warming, and livestock farming often involves the destruction of forests.

THE FUTURE
In the future, I will continue to change as wind, water, and ice erode rocks and soil and wash sediment into streams. This has always happened and it's perfectly natural.
Nothing changes!

But the natural forces of erosion don't only transport sediment to different places. They also carry human waste products.

Take plastic, for example. Plastic takes hundreds of years to break down. As a result, millions of tons of plastic end up in the ocean, harming wildlife like me.

You can reduce plastic waste by recycling or reusing such plastic items as grocery bags and water bottles.

Farm waste, such as manure and pesticides, gets washed by the rain into watercourses and ends up contaminating rivers, lakes, and wetlands, harming wildlife.

The decisions we make and the way we live can have far-reaching consequences. Much like the forces that slowly shape Earth, a little can go a long way!

By not throwing out a plastic bag, you could be saving the life of a dolphin half a world away.

CAN YOU BELIEVE IT?!
The Congo River in Africa is the
world's deepest river.
The river bed is 720 feet (220 meters)
deep at its deepest point.

Rising to more than 2.5 miles
(4 kilometers) above sea level,
Mauna Loa in Hawaii is
the largest
active volcano
in the world.

Some dunes are called "singing dunes"
because they make a whistling sound
when the wind blows
over them!

The Ganges Delta,
where the Ganges
River meets the
Bay of Bengal
in South Asia,
is the
largest
river
delta
in the
world!

A glacier in Greenland called **Jakobshavn Isbrae** is the world's

fastest glacier.

It reaches a top speed of about 130 feet (40 meters) per day.

The Denman glacier in Antarctica flows over the top of a canyon that extends at least 11,000 feet (3,500 meters) below sea level—the

deepest land canyon in the world!

Indonesia has the

most active volcanoes

of any country on Earth. At least

139 active volcanoes

can be found there!

The most powerful earthquake

ever recorded occurred about 100 miles (160 kilometers) off the coast of Chile in South America on May 22, 1960. It triggered a tsunami that struck the town of Hilo, Hawaii.

WORDS TO KNOW

bank the rising ground bordering a river or stream.

carbon footprint the amount of carbon dioxide emitted due to the use of fossil fuels by a particular person, group, or activity.

cove a small bay.

crater a bowl-shaped opening, often found at the top of a volcano.

crest the highest points on a ripple, wave, ridge, or dune.

fissure a long, narrow opening or crack.

fossil fuels sources of energy that formed from the remains of living things that died millions of years ago. Coal, oil, and natural gas are fossil fuels.

gradient a slope.

hydroelectricity electric energy generated using the motion of falling or flowing water.

lava molten rock that pours out of volcanoes or from cracks in Earth.

load the total amount of sediment carried by a river or stream.

sedimentary rock rock formed by the accumulation and compression of layers of sediment over time.

tectonic plate a massive, irregular-shaped slab of rock, usually composed of continental and oceanic crust. Earth's surface is made up of about 30 tectonic plates.

trough the lowest point between ridges or dunes.

undulating rising and falling.

water table the level below which the ground is saturated with water.